Contents

Introduction

Snakes are fascinating animals so it's not surprising
that an increasing number of these reptiles are being
kept in terrariums. Fortunately our knowledge about
their care in captivity has increased enormously over
recent years. That applies also to the degree to which
they are being bred in captivity. This book is intended
for the beginner whom I hope it will enable to keep
these animals safely and possibly breed them.
The latter, by the way, is the most satisfying aspect
of this exciting hobby.

It's still unfortunately true, especially for a beginner
confronted with a comment like 'What in God's name
is the point of keeping those slimy creatures in a box?'
that prejudiced family members and friends will need
to be won over. The beginner will be able to use this
book hopefully also to convince any doubtful family
members of the beauty of these fascinating animals
and the pleasure they can give their keeper.

Jan-Cor Jacobs

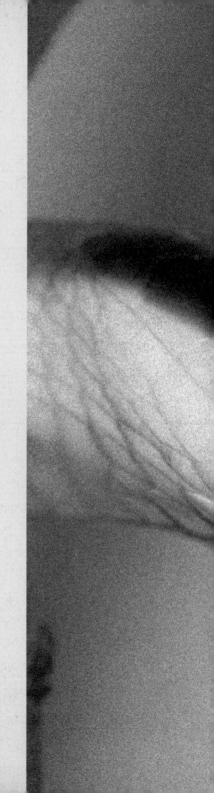

Jan-Cor **Jacobs**

ion, housing, care,

breeding and species

Contents

Elaphe taenivra ridleyi

A Publication of About Pets.

Copyright © 2003
About Pets
co-publisher United Kingdom
Kingdom Books
PO9 5TL, England

ISBN 1852792256
First printing
September 2003

Original title: *Slangen*
© 2002 Welzo Media Productions bv,
About Pets,
Warffum, the Netherlands
http://www.aboutpets.info

Photos:
European Snake Society
and Rob Doolaard

Printed in Italy

General

Snakes are long bodied legless animals. A few primitive varieties, such as the giant snakes, still have vestigial pelvis and hind limbs that are visible as spurs either side of the cloaca. Snakes have between 100 and 400 vertebrae that give them great flexibility of movement.

Emerald tree boa

Very strong muscles that run the length of the body are used to strangle prey or crawl. To move, snakes crawl with their belly scales or lever their muscled coils against the ground.

Many people think that snakes are slimy and slippery but the opposite is true. Depending upon the variety, the skin is dry and rough to the touch.

Predators

All snakes are predators but there are many snakes that become prey themselves to larger snakes. Depending upon the variety and the terrain in which they are found, they hunt actively or by laying in wait to ambush their victims. Snakes kill by two means: through strangulation or with venom. Constrictors grip their prey by wrapping their body around them. Each time the prey exhales the snake tightens its grip preventing it from inhaling, eventually suffocating it before the victim is finally swallowed.

Venomous snakes inject poison with a quick bite. If death or paralysis is not immediate the snake uses its acute sense of smell to locate its victim once it has died or become paralysed. Snakes have special jaws and floating ribs that allow them to swallow prey much larger than themselves.

Senses

Snakes smell by using their forked tongue to collect scent molecules and pass them to a special sensor. They have no external ear openings or inner ear but they can sense sound vibrations, especially through the ground. Most reptiles have good eyesight but the snake's eyelids have developed into an immoveable transparent scale so snakes can't actually see very well. They do however have an acute sense of smell.

A number of giant snakes have special heat sensitive grooves in their lips. Some varieties even have an organ that can detect small differences in temperature to help to locate prey in the dark. Many of these snakes hunt to their best advantage at night.

Snakes breath with their lungs. With the exception of giant snakes the right lung is normally underdeveloped. Because they can store an air supply in a rear sac-like lung, snakes can remain underwater for a long time (up to 30 minutes). Many snakes are good swimmers.

Elaphe schrencki

Lampropeltis getulus californiae (albino variety)

Buying

As corny as it may sound, 'look before you leap' definitely applies to anyone considering keeping snakes.

The green mamba *(Dendroaspis angusticeps)* is a very dangerous poisonious snake and not suitable as a pet!

Tempting as it may be to keep a beautifully coloured snake in a terrarium, these animals need to be cared for so before buying one it's sensible to check if you're able to provide the animal with everything it needs.

Where to buy

As soon as the terrarium is prepared (see chapter Housing), you're ready to buy your animals. You can obtain them at a specialised pet shop or through an amateur breeder, although buying through an amateur breeder does have several advantages:

- You can look at the parents to get a good idea of the size and colour your own animal will eventually be.
- More importantly, you will be able to see if the parents are healthy.

- The breeder will be able to tell you how often the animal eats and what it eats.
- The price will be substantially cheaper than buying from a specialised pet shop.

One disadvantage is that the animals are generally very young and more physically vulnerable than juveniles or adults.

Bred or caught in the wild

If you're buying from a shop always ask if the snakes have been bred or caught in the wild. The latter can cause a lot of problems. They may for example be carrying parasites or refuse food. Animals bred in snake farms are often infested with parasites. Ball pythons *(Python regius)*, especially, will often have been bred at this type of farm in West Africa.

Inspection tips

Before handing over your money, it's sensible to give the animal a good inspection:

- The snake should rapidly flick its tongue when something is held in front of it.
- There should be no space between the scales and there should be no traces of the remains of moulting.
- The eyes should be clear. If the eyes are dull or milky it may be a sign that the animal will be moulting within the next few days. In this case buy the animal only after it has shed its skin.
- The jaws should close well and the snake shouldn't feel too limp when handled.
- Don't buy an animal that's lying stretched out in the terrarium and not alert.

Ball python
(Python regius)

Transport

Use a strong sealed linen bag to transport large snakes. Smaller snakes are best moved in a plastic box lined with damp tissue paper, such as a closed sandwich box, sealed with tape. Don't forget though to ensure that there are sufficient ventilation holes in the

The African house snake *(Lamprophis fuliginosus)* is one of the easiest to breed. Here a hatchling emerges from the egg.

lid and that they are smaller in diameter than the snake.

Handling

One of the most important principles is very simple: although a snake will occasionally need to be removed from its terrarium, it should be removed as little as possible. Lightly grasp it and support the body with both hands. Small snakes are very delicate and can best be grasped in the middle with two fingers. An aggressive snake should be held directly behind it's head to ensure that it can't bite. You can also throw a cloth over the animal to disorientate it before attempting to grasp it. If necessary, use a special snake hook.

Dangerous or venomous snakes such as adders rattlesnakes and cobras are not dealt with in this book. Only very experienced and specialised snake keepers should keep these animals.

Bites

Anybody working with snakes will get bitten now and again. If you're frightened of getting bitten, it's a good idea to get some experience with a keeper first. Remember, it's not the snake's fault if you're too frightened to clean its Terrarium!

Snakebites are generally not painful, but this depends on the size of the animal. The reaction of most people who get bitten in the hand, which is the most common place for keepers to be bitten, is to instinctively jerk the hand back. A snake's fangs curve inward so the instinctive reaction just makes the wound larger, so try to avoid doing it. Hold the bitten hand still and use your free hand to open the animal's jaws by lightly applying finger pressure behind the jaws. It's normally quite easy.

Snakes attempt to bite most often during feeding. They will bite at anything that moves once they smell food. When you are taking the animal out of its terrarium, or replacing its water for example, make sure that your hands don't smell of food. When feeding aggressive snakes a protective glove can be worn on the hand used to offer the food to the snake.

Red-tailed green ratsnake *(Gonyosoma oxycephala)*

The rattle of a rattlesnake

Housing

Terrariums can be obtained in all varieties and sizes, but you can of course build one yourself to suit your own tastes. The terrarium will be the snake's permanent living accommodation so it's important that the interior reproduces the snake's natural habitat. This differs by snake variety so make sure you obtain sound advice before you obtain one.

Most snakes should have the possibility to climb.
Here is a *Elaphe taeniura friesei*

A terrarium takes up space, especially when keeping large pythons and boas. It's also more difficult to furnish than for example an aquarium. Any live plants used in a natural terrarium will have short lives. If they don't wilt in the heat they may well die under the weight of the animal.

With the right care some varieties can live in excess of 20 years so it's important for anyone embarking on this hobby to realise that a snake is not a short-term commitment.

Size

If what's gone before hasn't raised any insurmountable problems, the terrarium can be obtained taking into account the variety of snake you're intending to keep. Tree dwellers need a taller terrarium than ground dwellers. All terrariums need to be placed in a draught free, stable location.

There are differing theories about size. One theory says that for ground dwelling snakes the floor diagonal of the terrarium should be 0.7 to 1 times the length of the animal. For tree dwellers the same requirement applies but to the height diagonal of the terrarium also.

Another calculation method states that the length of the box must be a minimum of two thirds of the length of the snake, and the width and height a minimum of one third. For tree dwellers the length of the box must be a minimum of two thirds of the length of the snake, the width one third and the height two thirds. There is no specific rule. However, a small and well-furnished terrarium is generally better than a large one not furnished to meet the snake's basic requirements.

Ready to use terrariums are available in all sizes at specialist pet shops but many snake keepers make their own boxes from glass and wood. You can also convert an old aquarium by adding a top and some ventilation strips. Working in a box from above creates more stress for the animals than working from the front so, for anyone who has a choice, a terrarium with sliding front doors is the best solution.

Another important point regardless of the solution chosen is security. Snakes are real Houdini's at wriggling their way through narrow splits and tiny holes. The most popular terrariums have two sliding glass doors at the front. Between the doors is a vertical gap. Newly born snakes can crawl through but the gap is too small for larger animals. Nevertheless, it's sensible to fit the doors with a display-case lock to prevent a snake sliding open a door with its nose.

Heating

Terrariums sold in specialist pet shops usually have one or more lamp fittings. Lamps can be used to provide light and a sunny spot for the animals to warm themselves

Agkistrodon contortrix, beautifull but poisonious

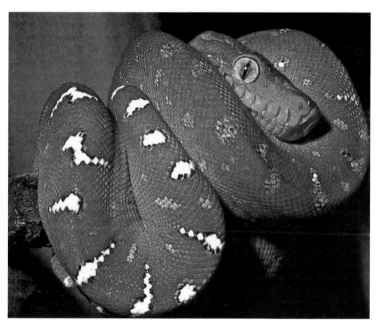

Corallus caninus is a typical tree dweller. The young are often a completely different colour than the parents. This variety of tree dwelling boa needs a relatively high terrarium.

Author's own experience!!!
I've been surprised in a corridor at my home by young Viperine Grass Snakes that escaped from an apparently closed terrarium.
The place where the heating cable entered the terrarium was neatly sealed and yet the animals had still been able to get out! After much searching I finally discovered their route through a small crack next to a hinged door. Even though the crack was much smaller than the diameter of the animals they had been able to wriggle their way through. Plenty of other snake enthusiasts have similar stories.

in but it's important they can't burn themselves. So never place a twig, branch or other support in the area of any lamp.

The floor can be warmed with heating mats and cables that are available in various sizes and wattages. Snakes regulate their body temperature by moving between warm and cold areas so it's important that the floor heat source never covers the entire floor area of the terrarium. It's also a good idea to connect them to a thermostat to ensure that the temperature doesn't get too high.

Furnishing

Furnishing a terrarium depends entirely on the variety of snake it's designed for but all snakes have certain basic needs. A hide box is essential. These can be made of tree bark or an upturned flowerpot with an entrance hole cut into it. Branches and stones can also be used. No matter what's used, it's important that everything is fixed firmly in its place and that nothing can be dislodged. Snakes are very strong animals and they can apply a substantial amount of force with their bodies. Fallen branches and stones can lead to injury and breakages in the terrarium.

In addition to a hiding place, clean water needs to be available. Most snakes like to bathe so the water dish should be big enough for the snake to soak in coiled up. Many animals unfortunately also like to use it as a toilet. The water will need to be changed daily so it's important that the dish be located in an easily accessible part of the terrarium.

As far as substrate (floor cover) is concerned, terrarium keepers' opinions differ. Some swear by old newspapers.
Whilst they are not pretty to look at, they do have the advantage of being easy to replace once soiled with faeces.

Wood shavings and wood chips are a good alternative. A terrarium with a wood chip covered floor is nicer to look at than one lined with newspapers. Peat is also sometimes used. The disadvantage of peat however, especially with fish-eating snakes, is that it can easily stick to the food and be swallowed by the snake together with the food. This needs to be avoided at all costs.

A swimming
Nerodia fasciata

Diet

With the exception of egg-eating snakes, snakes in the wild eat live prey. Some varieties are highly specialised in eating snails for example. Most varieties kept in terrariums eat rodents and fish but in captivity some can even get used to swallowing dead prey.

Dead prey

You can easily breed mice and rats yourself in a laboratory cage, however be aware that this method of food production takes up more time than caring for the snakes. For somebody with only a few animals it's better to contact another snake keeper who already breeds mice and obtain a supply when it's required. Many specialist pet shops supply frozen mice and rats in various sizes. It goes without saying that these need to be allowed to thaw first. Place them for five minutes or so in hot, not boiling, water and they can be fed to the animals still wet. Most snakes will eat them quite readily. The disadvantage is that wet mice don't smell much like prey. The scent is retained better if they are allowed to thaw slowly in a warm place, if you can stand the smell! Mice should never be defrosted in a microwave oven, unless of course you were planning to give the oven a good clean anyway.

Live prey

Live prey is the favourite of many animals but feeding with live prey has one or two disadvantages. For one, most people can't bear the thought of watching a cuddly mouse being captured, strangled and eaten by a snake.

For the snake enthusiast, though, it's important to realise that a rodent is equally capable of injuring its predator so it's wise to keep an eye on things during feeding. If the snake doesn't appear to be interested in the prey, remove the prey from the terrarium.

Never leave live mice or rats in a terrarium at night because there is a real possibility that they will bite the sleeping snake and seriously injure it.

Fish eaters

Fish eaters can be fed with fish such as guppies or small goldfish. Guppies are easy to breed and goldfish can be bought at all pet shops. Frozen fish can be used but over time this can result in a vitamin B1 deficiency in fish-eating snakes that causes them to lose control of their bodies and eventually die. Frozen fish also need to be defrosted and vitamins should be added regularly to compensate for any potential B1 deficiency. Whole fish are preferable to fillets. Frozen smelt are excellent and available in many specialist pet shops.

Prey in general

Snakes eat comparatively large prey but don't give them food that's too large. The prey should not be much thicker than the thickest part of the snake.

Because their prey is comparatively large, a snake doesn't need to feed very often. Having eaten, boas and pythons may not find it necessary to eat again for a month. Fish digests quicker than meat, so it's sensible to feed fish eaters more often, twice a week for example. Other snakes are satisfied with one meal per week

during which they may eat two or three mice. The amount depends upon the size of the prey and naturally on the size of the snake itself. In the mating season and after laying eggs, females need more food than normal to regain their strength. Males by contrast, having other priorities, don't eat. Animals that are about to moult often refuse food.

Small fish are suitable as feed for fisheating snakes

It's sensible to separate animals during feeding. I use so called Fauna Boxes. These are small, plastic terrariums. If animals aren't separated there's a good chance that two or more snakes will start eating the same prey. Because the fangs are curved inward its difficult for snakes to let go once they have started feeding and its possible that one of the snakes will get eaten together with the prey. If two animals start eating the same mouse you'll need to force one of them to let go as quickly as possible. If carefully applying finger pressure just behind the jaws fails to open them then more extreme measures are necessary. Press an alcohol-soaked rag against the nose of one of the snakes, for example, and it will let go.

Poor eaters

Snakes are not always enthusiastic eaters. They refuse food occasionally because it's the mating season or they are about to shed their skin. Many snakes refuse food

African soft furred rats *(Praomys natalensis)*, also known as multimammate mouse or rat, give birth to lots of young and are very suitable as prey for snakes

because they have reached the hibernation period.
A snake can also refuse to eat without any apparent reason. There is no reason to panic but its important to check the animal daily. It could be that it's bothered by parasites or suffering from stress. Maybe the temperature and humidity are not optimal.

If terrarium conditions are favourable and the animal still refuses to eat, one solution is to offer alternative food. It's known for example that King Pythons prefer to eat Multimammate mice (Mastomys natalensis) rather than ordinary mice.

Box of tricks
I had to use all sorts of tricks to get a pair of Hognose snakes (Heterodon nasicus) eating again. In the wild, these animals hunt toads but these can't be provided

for them in captivity. Fortunately they are not too choosy and will eat mice in a terrarium...according to books at least. The snakes I'd bought were wild-caught and they'd been eating a mouse per week while living with the supplier. After an acclimatisation period of two weeks or so in their new accommodation, I offered them their first food but they turned up their noses.

After a week, I tried again with the same result. After two months I had to resort to the box of tricks:
- First I put the snakes into a plastic box containing small dead mice and closed the lid for a few hours. This common method unfortunately didn't have the desired effect.
- Then I tried something less pleasant a few times. I put the snakes into the plastic box again - with sufficient ventilation of course - together with the prey. This time however the heads of the dead mice had been cut open. You need to press softly on the open head so that a little brain fluid leaks on to the body of the mouse. Irresistible apparently... except for my Hognose snakes.
- In the end I simply had to trick them. Snakes that hunt in the wild for prey that we can't offer them in captivity will often eat other prey as long as it smells like their natural food. The

Madagascar boa

Hognose snakes simply needed to be offered mice with toad scent. At the pet shop I asked for some water from a terrarium containing toads. I dipped thawed-out mice in the water and then held them in front of the snakes with tweezers. They lunged immediately.

• I used the trick again and they started to eat mice as though they were their natural food.

Forced feeding

If feeding tricks don't help and the animal is visibly losing weight there is no other choice than to start forced feeding. The animal should be grasped behind its head and the body held as straight as possible. The snake will often open its jaws as a defence mechanism, if not you will have to carefully force them open with a spatula. The food can be placed in the jaws with blunt tweezers and carefully pushed inside using a smooth rounded probe. Once the prey has been pushed far enough inside the snake's body, it needs to be softly massaged down to the stomach. The stomach of a snake is located about one-third along its body length.

It's not necessary to use the normal food for forced feeding. In fact it's better to give something that's easily digestible and can be given with a syringe or a pipette, for example. There are various recipes for purées available that often include egg yolk, lean beef or fish. It's advisable though to add a vitamin preparation specially made for reptiles.

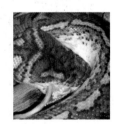

Anatomy

To keep terrarium snakes in healthy condition, a keeper needs to have a basic knowledge of snake anatomy. For many people snakes are slippery animals without legs.

Cave ratsnake
(Elaphe taeniura ridleyi)

The latter is correct but only in part, the former is a prejudice. All snakes have scales. Many boas and pythons have spurs or vestigial legs either side of the cloaca. Partly for this reason they are regarded as primitive snakes. The left lung in the majority of boa and python varieties still functions, but in nearly all other snakes it has withered or has disappeared completely.

The snake's stomach is relatively large. In some varieties it can take up to a third of the total body length. There is no urinary bladder: unlike mammals, snakes excrete no urine.

Males have no penis but a so-called hemipenes. This is a penis that's divided in a left and a right half. The form can differ by variety. Some have spines, while others have hooks to be able to firmly anchor themselves to the cloaca of the female during mating.

Prey are eaten whole without being bitten in pieces or chewed. Snakes are able to open their jaws very wide thanks to the flexibility of the quadrate bone. This bone acts as a double-jointed hinge between the upper jaw and the lower jaw that do not directly connect with each other. The lower jaw is divided into two halves that can move independently of each other. Anybody who keeps snakes will often see their animals pulling strange faces: when yawning a snake's lower jaw can ripple like a wave.

Vertebra

The number of vertebra is enormous and varies between 100 in Adders to more than 300 in Ring Snakes and exceeding 400 in large Pythons. All vertebrae support ribs and all ribs are flexible because they are not connected to a breastbone. This flexibility is essential if a large prey is to be swallowed.

Senses

Snakes have no ears. 'Hearing' is in fact done through the body sensing vibrations. This is one of the most important reasons that snakes are not often seen in the wild. They feel us approaching long before we arrive and have time to hide.

Snakes smell by using their forked tongue to pick up scent molecules in the air. The tongue is repeatedly brought into contact with the openings of two small channels on the roof of the mouth leading to a scent analyser (Jacobson's organ). Glands located at the opening of these channels excrete a fluid that transports the molecules to the analyser where the snake actually smells the scent.

Moulting

One of the most obvious characteristics of snakes is that they regularly shed their skins. The dead skin layer of the epidermis (outer skin) does not grow with the snake and is normally shed com-

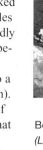

Boelen's python
(Liasis boeleni)

Cuban boa
(Epicrates angulifer)

East Dunbartonshire Coun

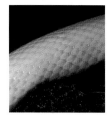

plete. The old skin layer loosens first around the jaws. The snake then rubs its snout against wood, stone and other rough objects to further loosen it. The skin normally rolls off like a stocking, inside out but it's advisable for terrarium keepers to check. While it's possible that the skin may tear naturally in the process, if it's not shed complete this may indicate that the snake is not in good condition.

A peeling snake

Scales

Snakes have scales. The number and the form vary by variety and are often used to determine the variety. Because the scales on the head differ in form to scales on the back or on the belly they have their own name. Writers in magazines and books for terrariums keepers conjure with these names, so for the uninitiated they are often complete Double-Dutch. The most

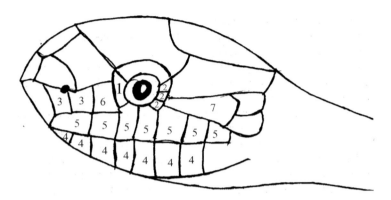

important and most used are listed below.

- Preocular: Scale in front of the eye (1)
- Postocular: Scales behind the eye (2)
- Post/Prenasal: Scales surrounding the nasal passage (3)
- Lower labials: Lower lip scales (4)
- Upper labials: Upper lip scales (5)
- Loreal: Scale between the preocular and the nasal scales (6)
- Temporal: Scale behind the orbit (7)
- Rostral: Scale above the snout (8)
- Frontal: Scale in the middle of the head, between the supraocular scales (9)
- Internasal: Scale behind the rostral scale (10)
- Prefrontal: Scales between the Internasal and the frontal scales (11)
- Supraocular: Scales above the eyes (12)
- Parietal: Behind the eyes (13)

- Ventral: Belly scales
- Dorsal: Back scales
- Anal shield: Scale around the cloaca. This scale can be divided or undivided
- Subcaudal: Scales under the tail

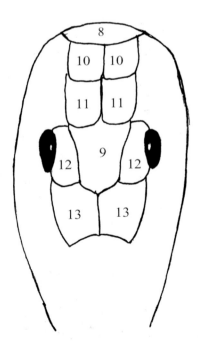

Reproduction

Many terrarium keepers not only strive to keep their animals alive and healthy as long as possible, they want to breed them as well. To do this it's naturally necessary to obtain at least one male and female of the same variety first.

A python hatchling

Sexing

Sexing can be done in different ways but not every method is equally reliable. In adult animals, the females are often bigger and have shorter tails than the males.

The tail root in males where the tail starts to taper is thicker than in females. But to be sure you need to compare animals of a similar age brought up under more or less identical circumstances.

Juvenile snakes can be "popped'. By applying pressure to the underside of the tail root the hemipenes can be everted. This method of sexing can lead to injury to the animal and should only be done by experienced keepers!

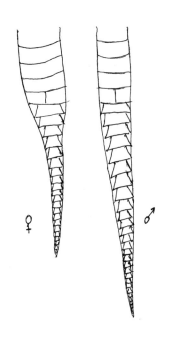

♀   ♂

Another reliable and popular way is by probing by an expert. The animal needs to be kept still, which is an art in itself! A sterilised and lubricated ball-tipped probe is very carefully introduced into the cloaca. The probe is then very carefully inserted further either on the right or left side in the direction of the tail. The probe can be inserted further into males than in females where a paired musk gland blocks its path. The male will sometimes tense itself during probing to the extent that the probe cannot be inserted deeply enough whereby the animal may be incorrectly sexed as a female.

Mating
The genitals of the male are divided in two halves. During mating the left or the right hemipenes project outwards. During intercourse the hemipenes is often so firmly anchored in the cloaca of the female that the male is dragged around the terrarium. A shock reaction by the female can result in the male being seriously injured so they should not be disturbed during mating.

Mating by animals living in moderate climate zones normally takes place following hibernation. This often happens after a female has shed her skin. When the animals are ready to mate, the males often refuse all food whereas the females actually require more food.

Egg laying
We learn at school that snakes, like all other reptiles, lay eggs. About a quarter of all varieties

however give birth to live young. In these varieties, to which Boa's and Garter snakes belong, the eggs are fully developed in the mother's body. No shell is formed but each embryo is covered in a clear membrane. The young hatch immediately the eggs are laid.

Most varieties lay eggs with soft leathery shells that hatch several weeks after they have been laid. Pregnant females will always try to lay their eggs in the most favourable place, in the terrarium. To prevent an animal from inad-

vertently laying her eggs in the water dish, or from simply sprea-ding them around the terrarium, a laying tray filled with damp peat or sphagnum moss should be pla-ced in a warm spot. The animal will almost certainly use it.

Incubator

Terrariums conditions are not ideal for hatching eggs so the clutch will need to be transferred to an incubator. When doing so the eggs must never be turned because there is a risk that the foetus will die. Although profes-

Western Hognose Snake *(Heterodon nasicus)* emerges from its egg

Author's own experience
I use a small terrarium that I place on a heating mat. A thermostat ensures that the temperature remains constant. The eggs are placed in a ventilated closed box that's supported on one side by a small block. Standing the box at an angle ensures that water condensation from the lid drips very little if at all on the eggs.

sional incubators are available they are expensive so it really only makes sense to buy one if you are intending to incubate a lot of reptile eggs.

A simple hatching alternative is the 'au bain marie' method. Take an (old) aquarium, partly fill it with water and warm the water using an aquarium heater coupled to a thermostat. Place a tray containing the reptile eggs on a raised platform in the water. Make sure that the young snakes cannot escape from the tray or they are certain to drown as soon as soon as they hatch!

The eggs can best be placed on a vermiculite (used in plant cultivation), sphagnum moss or peat substrate but they must not be buried. The substrate should be damp but not wet. The proportion of water to vermiculite should be 1:1. After wetting, the peat and sphagnum moss should be wrung out. Dry the substrate around and under the eggs and moisten it again carefully with tepid water. A substrate that's too wet can lead to the eggs absorbing too much water and the embryos will die.

During incubation, the air humidity must remain constant at between 80 and 100 percent. The temperature should not be allowed to fluctuate significantly. That said, cases are known of eggs hatching even after the temperature has dropped substantially during incubation.

The German snake keeper Friedrich Golder carried out experiments to see if low temperatures were inevitably fatal. He used a clutch of Viperine Grass Snake eggs. The Viperine Grass Snake, Natrix maura, can be found, amongst other places, in France and Spain. The eggs were hatched at a temperature of between 66 and 68 degrees F (19 and 20 degrees C) in fifteen weeks. In the fifth week the lamp being used as

Elaphe guttata with eggs

Author's own experience
I happened to have eggs from an African Egg Eating Snake *(Dasypeltis medici medici)*. Unfortunately during that period the power failed on a few occasions whereby the temperature dropped to about 68 degrees F (20 degrees C). Of the four eggs one hatched and produced a healthy specimen.

Elaphe
taeniura
ridleyi

the heat source failed. Golder increased the temperature again only in the ninth week. During the cold period the eggs gained little or no weight but the embryos did not die. The young finally emerged after 106 days. At an incubation temperature of 75 degrees F (24 degrees C) the incubation time is shorter by half, namely 53 days.

Young snakes

Keepers of Garter Snakes and other snakes that lay live young can be surprised to suddenly find a teeming mass of baby snakes in the terrarium. With these types of snakes, it's better to place pregnant animals apart in a simply furnished maternity terrarium. It's easier to catch the young animals, and other snakes don't bother them. Young animals can best be reared in small boxes individually or, if necessary, in small groups. In the latter case animals of the same size should be placed together and an eye kept on proceedings during feeding time, or they might start eating each other! Rearing animals individually saves them at the very least a lot of stress. It's also easier to identify those that are eating well and those that are not. The temperature should be the same as for more mature animals, but the humidity can be a little higher. This is important if moulting is to take place normally. This does not mean however that young snakes should be housed in a damp or even wet terrarium. This can lead to other troubles such as scale rotting.

A Corn snake (Elaphe guttata) lays her eggs in a specially provided tray.

The Ball python
(Python regius)
incubates its eggs:
The female hatches
her eggs.

Juveniles don't eat until after they have shed their skin for the first time. After that, they need to be offered prey of the appropriate size. It often happens that juveniles refuse food initially. In this case hold the food with a pair of tweezers and wave it back and forth in front of the snake's snout. The animal will most likely lunge at the food a couple of times and finally accept it.

Should this be unsuccessful, place the snake and the food together in a small closed box, a clean margarine carton or a salad box for example. If the food is a dead baby mouse it may help if the skull is slightly opened to allow

some brain fluid to escape. Forced feeding should only be used in extreme cases.

Feed young snakes more often than adult animals, but don't overfeed them or digestion problems may arise. If juveniles eat well, they will of course grow quickly. Young Corn Snakes (Elaphe guttata) can double their weight in 1.4 to 2.2 months but the older animals get, the less they grow. A young python, for example, grew an average of 3 inches (7.6 centimetres) per month in the first two years of its life. From its second to its fourteenth year, the animal only grew by 42 inches (107 centimetres).

Corallus caninus

Hibernation and Brumation

Snakes living in moderate climates rest (called brumation) and sleep (called hibernation) in the winter. Animals resting remain active to some degree as temperatures drop but there is little activity if any during sleep or hibernation.

Trinket snake
(Elaphe helena)

Snakes kept in terrariums have the same needs. Most varieties are likely to remain healthy even if they don't have this cooling down period, however it's to the snake's advantage to follow a natural cycle. Many animals reproduce better as a result.

Preparation

A few rules need to be followed if animals are to winter successfully.

- It's important to stop feeding well in advance to ensure that the intestines are completely empty before hibernation begins. Food remaining won't be digested at low temperatures and will rot leading to the animal's death. Animals in a poor physical condition should not be allowed to hibernate since they may die as a result.

- Start reducing the temperature and the lighting time of the terrarium approximately two weeks after the last feed. This can best be done in stages over a period of 14 days or so, at the end of which the lighting time should be down to a couple of hours a day. The temperature can be reduced in a box heated by lamps by fitting lamps of a lower wattage.

- The animals can now be transferred to their hibernation box. This can be a small terrarium or another suitable ventilated box. When temperatures are very low, the hibernation box should be placed in a cellar or in an attic for example to avoid frost damage. Some enthusiasts even hibernate their animals in the refrigerator. Drinking water needs to be available and the box needs to be checked regularly. The animals should also be able to dig themselves into the substrate. Peat dust is suitable. Sawdust can also be used. Six to eight weeks of hibernation is sufficient for most varieties, but for those from areas where winters are normally longer and more severe the hibernation period can be increased to as much as four months.

Activity

As the time approaches to stimulate the animals back into activity they can be returned to their regular accommodation and the temperature and the lighting time gradually increased. Once the temperature has returned to normal, it's time to start feeding the snakes again. Since most start to eat only after the first moult following

hibernation, they may initially refuse food. Males may also refuse food because of paying more attention to the opposite sex.

Oxybelis fulgidus

Health and sicknesses

However good the care is, sicknesses are unfortunately unavoidable. Prevention is naturally always better than a cure so never place new animals directly into a terrarium where other snakes live.

Red-tailed green ratsnake
(Gonyosoma oxycephala)

If a newcomer is sick or carries parasites, there is a high risk that the other animals will become infected. Always place newcomers in a sparsely furnished quarantine terrarium for a few weeks. If a snake is sick contact the vet, don't play doctor yourself. The following summary of sicknesses and complaints is far from complete and serves only as an indication of what a snake keeper can expect if there is a setback.

Parasites

Parasites are small animals that live off other animals or a so-called host. Whilst not sick in themselves these animals can make their host very sick (pathogens). The majority of parasites suck the host's blood, weakening it.

External parasites

These are parasites that live on the outside (in and on the skin) of the snake. Snakes can suffer from mites and ticks. Mites have the appearance of dark red to black specks that crawl through the terrarium and over the snake. Snakes suffering from mites lay in water more than normal. Drowned mites float on the surface of the water.

If mites are present in the terrarium there is no alternative other than to dispose of the furnishings and thoroughly disinfect the box. The parasites will also be present in the area in which the terrarium is kept so it's advisable to hang up a few Vapona-strips in the same room. The terrarium can best be cleaned with trichlorfon in a concentration of between two and five percent. The animals should be placed in a trichlorfon moistened cotton bag for 24 hours or so. This is not without risk however. Some young snakes' reflexes disappear for a few days and they may show signs of uncontrolled head shaking.

Ticks are substantially larger than mites and can be removed by twisting them out. Make sure that the head of the tick is also removed.

Internal parasites
Internal parasites are difficult to diagnose. Wild-caught snakes occasionally suffer from flagellate. These single celled organisms are only visible under the microscope. Snakes that refuse food and that vomit or have slimy faeces may be carriers. If the snake refuses food and there are signs of blood in the faeces, amoeba may be the cause. In either case you should consult a specialist vet. Reduced appetite, loss of weight and diarrhoea can be caused by other single-celled organisms: coccidia. The symptoms called coccidiosis can result in serious intestinal infections. It's important to pay a visit to the vet in these cases also.

If you can't identify the parasite you are dealing with, you can have a specimen of the faeces analysed by the vet. The specimen must be less than 24 hours old when it's analysed.

Fungus infections
Fungus infections *(mycoses)* are not often seen in snakes. An external infection often starts on the belly scales *(ventrals)* and is identifiable as brownish spots. The infection can spread to the back and even affect the eyes. Treatment is possible using a special anti-fungal ointment that can be obtained from the vet.

Abscesses
A snake may occasionally suffer from one or more abscesses or tumours. In this case a vet will need to treat them surgically.

Stromatitus
A relatively frequent sickness is Stomatitus. This sickness occurs mostly when a snake has been kept in poor conditions over a long period of time. Small white to yellowish specks on pale gums are often the first visible symptom. A cheese-like mould of dead tissue forms in the mouth. At a later stage teeth may fall out and even jaw and bone tissue can become infected.

Treat Stromatitus as early as possible. Remove dead tissue with a cotton bud that's been soaked in a 3% hydrogen peroxide solution. A course of antibiotics should be given in consultation with the vet. Giving extra vitamin A and C can stimulate the healing process. If the snake recovers well, the

A tick

Albino Burmese python *(Python molurus bivittatus)*

*Lampropeltis
getulus californiae,
albino variety*

Eunectes notaeus

mucus tissue in mouth will
regenerate, as will the teeth.

Poxes

Pox is a collective name for a
group of infections that take the
form of blisters on the skin. They
can appear if a terrarium is too
damp or cold. Even snakes that
normally live in wet areas, such as
Garter Snakes, are liable to the
infection. Fistula bumps or
blisters can indicate the presence
of pox. Unfortunately, it's not
always clear which pathogen has
caused the pox so that specific
treatment is not possible. An
infected animal can sometimes

recover simply by being transferred
to a drier and warmer terrarium.

Breathing problems

If the snake has breathing problems, a draught will be the most
likely cause. Left untreated the
animal can develop pneumonia.
Place the snake as quickly as possible in a quarantine terrarium
with a constant   temperature of
between 82.5 and 86 degrees F
(28 and 30 degrees C).

Paramyxo virus

One of the most feared viruses
that affect snakes is the paramyxo
virus. Any animal can be a carrier

even without showing signs of the sickness. The virus will only reveal itself in snakes that are in poor physical condition. Symptoms can be diverse, from refusing food to breathing problems, secretion of fluid at the back of the throat, pneumonia, abnormal behaviour and even balance problems. Unfortunately, the symptoms are not always obvious and an outbreak might only be noticed when one or more snakes are suddenly found dead in the terrarium. A specialist vet should be called in even if there is only a suspicion of a paramyxo virus infection.

Problems with moulting

If a snake's skin has not been shed completely, it's possible that the terrarium is too dry. A healthy snake should be able to shed the remainder of its skin itself if the humidity is temporarily increased. Another effective solution is to bathe the snake in tepid water and let it crawl through a rough towel. Special attention should be given to ensure that no old skin remains around the eyes or the tail. If old skin is allowed to remain at the tip of the tail it can result in the tail dying off. Remains of old skin around the eyes can be removed carefully with tweezers.

Dendroaspis viridis peeling

The law

Sooner or later, terrarium keepers will be confronted with the laws concerning the keeping of animals. Of great importance are the CITES Convention and the CITES Lists. CITES stands for:

*Pituophis
melanoleucus*

'Convention on International Trade in Endangered Species of Wild Fauna and Flora', and it defines amongst other things which animals may and may not be traded, transported or kept in captivity.

The CITES lists summarise plants and animals that are under threat in the wild. There are four lists: A, B, C and D. The A-list details animals and plants that are under threat of extinction. Animals listed may be kept only under exceptional circumstances and it is forbidden to trade in them. The B-list details varieties of which trade is strictly controlled. Species on the C-list are endangered in one or a few countries and have been included at the request of that country or those countries that already regulate trade in the spe-

cies and need the cooperation of other countries to prevent exploitation. An import permit is required for these animals. This applies also to the varieties on the D-list of which the European Union wants to know the origin.

Its possible to obtain an exemption to keep animals in the B, C and D-lists. At the time of sale, the dealer is required to hand over a copy of the CITES-form. If you buy a CITES-animal from a private person, you must ask to be provided with a signed transfer statement that shows the appropriate CITES-number. Should you have any questions, please contact the CITES office.

Varieties of snakes

Of more than 2900 snake varieties, only a few are kept in terrariums. That's not surprising because not all varieties are attractive and some have very special requirements for example where food is concerned (termite eating snakes) and are not suitable for amateurs.

Red-tailed green ratsnake *(Gonyosoma oxycephala)*

Although some enthusiasts keep venomous snakes, I have not included them in this book. Venomous snakes place special demands on the keeper and are not suitable for a beginner.

Nomenclature

Like all other animals snakes have a scientific name built up out of two to three elements, the genus, the species, and the subspecies. For the enthusiast it's advisable to have the scientific names of the most common terrarium animals to hand. Scientific names are used in popular scientific literature and terrarium magazines to avoid misunderstandings.

Many varieties (certainly the sub species) don't have an English name. Additionally, for the snake enthusiast who is able to read foreign language magazines and books the popular names can lead to considerable misunderstanding. Germans for example call the Yellow Rat Snake a Kükennatter and not a gelbe Rattenschlange, as the literal translation would be. Unless the scientific name (in this case *Elaphe obsoleta quadrivittata*) is used, things become very confusing for the unsuspecting reader. Unfortunately, scientific names remain the subject of scientific discussion and as a result are subject to change. Recent name changes though are nearly always reported in the relevant literature.

Scientific names are used as much as possible in addition to the English names in the following summary to help the reader in a small way to get used to them. Popular names are sometimes misleading, which is an additional reason to use them with caution. Only snakes that are relatively easy to keep and the most easily bred are listed in the summary. The most popular varieties without doubt belong the Boidae family, the Boa's and Pythons. These are often imposing snakes with beautiful markings and striking colours. Also included are one or two varieties of the Colubridae family. This is by far the largest family of snakes and of special interest in terrarium keeping.

Boa Constrictor
Of the boas the *Boa Constrictor* is undoubtedly the best known.

Appearance
The *Boa constrictor* is a large snake that can grow to lengths in excess of 195 in (5.0m). The record is 218 in (5.6m). Although on average they are, luckily, considerably smaller at between 78 in (2.0m) and 117 in (3.0m), they remain substantial snakes that require a very roomy terrarium. *Boa Constrictor* markings consist of about 25 dark bands (saddles) on a light brown background.

Distribution/Habitat
Widespread from Mexico to Argentina. Often lives close to water. Hides in the undergrowth during the day to go hunting at dusk.

Housing
It goes without saying that when you are furnishing the terrarium you need to take into account the weight of the animal. Make sure that well anchored thick branches are available for the animals to rest in. Shelves can be used in place of branches and stumps.

During the day the temperature should be between 77 and 89.5 degrees F (25 and 32 degrees C); under the spotlights it may even be allowed to rise to 95 degrees F (35 degrees C). Make sure that the animals can't burn themselves on the spotlights! It's also advisable to use floor heating because adults, especially, often remain at ground level. At night the temperature can be allowed to drop to between 68 and 71.5 degrees F (20 and 22 degrees C). Spray the terrarium regularly with tepid water and make sure that a large water dish is available for the animals to soak in.

Diet
Boa constrictors are voracious eaters and food is seldom a problem. Young boas eat mice, young rats, hamsters and day old chicks. Larger animals can easily swallow adult rats, guinea pigs and rabbits.

Breeding
Boa constrictors are often bred in captivity. It's not necessary to stimulate the animals to mate because they mate naturally throughout the

There are different sub-species of Boa Constrictor. This is *Boa constrictor ortonii*. Boas bare live young.

Ordinary
Boa contrictor

year. According to some enthusiasts, the animals mate more frequently if they are kept at a low temperature with a relative humidity of less than 70 percent over a period of six to twelve weeks. Opinions differ somewhat about the gestation period. According to one person it's 17 weeks, to another it's 42 weeks. Like all boas the *Boa constrictor* produces live young that are born covered in a membrane and from which they quickly try to escape. This has to be completed, incidentally, without the egg tooth that the young boa lacks. The birth can take several hours after which the mother is about four kilos lighter which is equivalent to about half of her total body weight. 20 to 30 young are generally born, exceptionally up to 60. They measure between 14 and 21.5 inches (35 and 55 cm) long and weigh between 1.5 and 3.5 oz (45 en 95 g). Many young remain attached by their umbilical cord and have to be cut free, so the keeper sometimes has to assist with the birth. The umbilical cord dries out and eventually falls off after a few days.

Rearing

The young snakes moult for the first time between one and three weeks following birth. Thereafter they can be feed for the first time with young mice, and, depending on the size of the snakes, possibly adult mice. The mother should be fed as soon as possible after giving birth to regain her strength.

With adequate feeding, the animals grow quickly and within three years are sexually mature. Some boa's can be very aggressive toward their keeper. Try to get these animals as used to contact with people as possible. Put on strong gloves and take the animal out of the terrarium for 10 – 15 minutes each day. After a while, once the animal behaves less aggressively, try it without gloves. Place the animal on your lap and lay your hands carefully over its head so that it gets used to the smell of your hands. If the animal continues to attack while you are attempting to handle it, it's possibly better to give up and accept the aggressive behaviour. *Boa Constrictors* fall under the CITES convention (List-B). To keep these animals you need to be in possession of the necessary documents.

Liachanura trivirgata en Liachanura roseofusca (Rosy Boa's)

It's not surprising that 'Rosy boas' are very popular in the U.S.A. because this small Boa variety make ideal terrarium animals. Rosy Boas grow to between 27.5 and 35.5 inches (70 and 90 cm) in length. Because of their small size, they don't need large boxes.

Appearance

Liachanura trivirgata differs in markings from *Liachanura roseofusca* where the lengthwise stripes in L. trivirgata are more clearly visible. Some herpetologists don't recognise *L. roseofusca* as an independent species and consider it a subspecies of *L. trivirgata*.

Lichanura
(trivirgata)
roseofusca]

Distribution/Habitat
These snakes originate from dry areas in the western part of North America.

Housing and environmental factors
The terrarium must be dry and they especially like mild floor heating. A daytime temperature of between 72 and 79 degrees F (22 and 26 degrees C) is adequate. Whilst this small Boa variety lives mainly at ground level, some branches need to be included in the terrarium so that they can sunbathe on them during the day.

Diet
Rodents (especially mice) and birds.

Behaviour
These are very docile animals that never attempt to bite. When threatened, they will roll themselves into a ball. This type of snake is mainly active at dusk and at night.

Breeding
Hibernation is recommended if this variety is to be kept and bred successfully. The gestation period is four months and the number of young varies between four and twelve. The young are comparatively large at between 10 and 12 inches (25 and 30 cm) in length.

Rearing
The young can be fed with young mice. *Liachanura* grow quickly and they can reach a length of

27.5 inches (70 cm) in one year. Growth slows after two years when they are sexually mature. Adult animals grow between 0.8 and 1.6 inches (2 and 4 cm) a year at most. A CITES licence is required to keep 'Rosy Boa's'.

Eryx colubrinus (Kenyan Sand Boa)
Sand Boas of the Eryx family are small constrictors that live reclusive lives. During the day, they hide under stones or bury themselves in the sand. They are nevertheless popular terrarium animals due to their interesting behaviour, compact size and attractive markings.

Appearance
Eryx colubrinus is possibly the most kept variety. The back and flanks are covered with dark brown and orange patches. The orange patches form a zigzag pattern on the back. The belly is grey to yellow grey. This variety does not grow much longer than about 27.5 inches (70 cm).

Distribution
Eryx colubrinus live in the steppes and dry areas of the north and northeast of Africa and the Arabian Peninsula. .

Housing
A substrate layer of fine sand is required to keep these animals successfully in a terrarium. This layer needs to be between 3 and 4 inches (7 and 10 cm) thick. The daytime substrate temperature needs to be

high enough to produce an air temperature of between 86 and 95 degrees F (30 and 35 degrees C). This can be achieved by fixing a heating pad to the underside of the terrarium. The heating can be switched off at night and the temperature allowed to drop considerably. It's easiest to operate if the heating pad is attached to a time clock.

Diet

This constrictor hunts lizards and small rodents. The kill is in typical boa style with the snake first biting into the prey to anchor itself, then wrapping its body around it to strangle it. The catch is swallowed headfirst.

Mice can best be given in the evening when hunting would normally take place in the wild. Live mice are caught with lightening speed but Sand Boas quite easily adjust to eating dead mice which can be offered to them using long handled tweezers.

Breeding

Enthusiasts often breed *Eryx colubrinus*. The sexes are generally separated for a period of time to get them aroused. Mating occurs mostly in the summer with birth following in the autumn. The number of young produced can be up to 15. They are mostly between 6.5 and 8 inches (16.5 and 20 cm)

Eryx colubrinus loveridgei is the most kept sub-species

long and weigh between 0.2 and 0.4 oz (5 and 9 g)

Rearing

Nestling mice can be offered immediately following the first moulting. Many young are able to capture and strangle the smallest mice. Young that refuse to eat create a big problem because forced feeding these small animals is practically impossible. A so-called pinky pump can offer a solution. Baby mice are reduced to a puree in a substantial sort of syringe. This food puree is then injected into the young Sand boas throat and carefully massaged down to the stomach.

Care of other Eryx varieties is the same as for the *Eryx colubrinus*. A CITES license if required for keeping Eryx varieties.

Python regius (Ball or Royal Python)

The Ball Python is one of the absolute toppers in terrarium keeping and belongs to one of the most widely kept snake varieties.

Appearance

Python regius is a small variety with especially attractive black and yellow-patched markings. The Royal Python grows to a maximum of 71 inches (1.80 m) in length but the majority substantially less with an average of 49 inches (1.25 m).

Distribution

Python regius can be found in West and Central Africa. The largest concentrations are in Ivory Coast, Ghana, Benin, Togo and Burkina Faso, where they live on the savannas and in the tropical forests. According to African snake catchers, the colours of animals from damper areas display more contrast than those from drier areas. Not surprisingly, the Ball Python is also found in cultivated areas, especially in cassava fields that are often teaming with rodents.

Housing

Being a tropical snake, the Ball Python needs high temperatures. During the daytime the temperature needs to be between 82.5 and 86 degrees F (28 and 30 degrees C). At night the temperature can be allowed to fall to 73.5 degrees F (23 degrees C). A heating element and thermostat should be used to ensure that the temperature does not fall too low. If the terrarium is allowed to cool at night to room temperature, the snakes could develop colds or even pneumonia over the long term.

Python regius is mainly a ground dweller however young animals especially like to climb so one or two branches need to be included in the terrarium. Royal Pythons like to make use of boxes lined with damp sphagnum moss. In the wild, Royal Pythons often live in

Veeltepelmuis

abandoned termite mounds that have the perfect climate: the humidity is high and the temperature is more or less constant.

A hide box with damp lining in the terrarium can be a good alternative to a termite mound. Wood chip and wood shavings are an ideal substrate. The water dish needs to be large enough for the animals to soak in. When the air humidity in the terrarium is high enough, *Python regius* will bathe rarely if at all. Animals that bathe nevertheless are often suffering from mites. These are easy to recognise as black specks floating on the surface of the water. See also the chapter Health and Sicknesses.

Diet
Rodents are their natural prey. Although the Ball Python is known for being a problem eater, this applies mainly to animals caught in the wild. Animals bred en-masse in West African snake farms for terrarium keepers in Europe and the USA are also known to stubbornly refuse any mice they are offered. Sometimes the only solution is forced feeding. It's sensible though to try other tricks first.

The Ball Python *(Python regius)* is an attractive, small python variety.

For most Ball Pythons a African furry rat, also known as Multimammate mouse *(Praomys) Mastomys natalensis)* is an irresistible snack. Feed the snakes in the evening. If this doesn't work place a live Multimammate mouse in a bucket and cover half the top with a plank. A hungry snake will often try to fish its prey out of the bucket.

Breeding
A short cooling-off period is needed to get the animals to mate. In West Africa, this is from early October until December. This colder period when no rain falls starts in the East (Benin) and moves westwards. The colder period can be reproduced in the terrarium by reducing the night temperature over the period of eight to twelve weeks to about 68 degrees F (20 degrees C). The daytime temperature should not be altered. Although the animals remain active they may accept food less readily than normal or even reject it. The latter can indicate the start of mating activity. To improve the chances of breeding it's a good idea to keep the sexes separated throughout the year and place the male with the female a few days after the beginning of the cooler period. Placing the female with the male does not always have the desired effect though. Often the female goes off on an extended inspection tour of her new accommoda-

tion while the hapless male attempts unsuccessfully to mate with her. From the start of gestation, Ball Python females exhibit typical behaviour by laying the rear one third of their body on its side.

Generally between four and twelve eggs are laid. Although the Python regius hatches her eggs by coiling her body around them its advisable to hatch them artificially. The eggs hatch in about 60 days at a temperature of 89.5 degrees F (32 degrees C). Python regius eggs are comparatively large. On average they measure 3 inches (7 to 8 cm) by 2 inches (4 to 5 cm) and weigh about 3.5 oz (100 g). In marked contrast to many other reptile eggs, Python regius eggs do not increase in size during incubation.

Fertilised eggs are snow white and have a soft shell. Eggs that are noticeably smaller than the rest and/or have a wax or beige like colour have not been fertilised and need to be removed very carefully otherwise they will start to become mouldy.

Rearing
Young Python regius are generally not difficult eaters and will eat their first mouse after the first moulting. In most cases this will be a juvenile mouse because young Ball Pythons are already about 15.5 inches (40 cm)

ong. These animals are sexually mature within about three years by which time they will measure about 39 inches (100 cm).

Sexing

Sexing can have its difficulties. In many python varieties, males have larger spurs than females. This is unfortunately not the case with *Python regius*. The spurs are the same size in both sexes. The male's tail is a fraction longer than the female's and gets smaller more gradually than that of the female but a good comparison is only possible if a number of more or less the same size of animals is available.

Only probing will provide confirmation of the sex. In males the probe can be inserted between nine and twelve scale lengths, in females four to a maximum of seven. Probing may only be carried out by very experienced enthusiasts or by a vet. If carried out by an inexperienced or an untrained person, animals can suffer internal injury.

Availability

A number of colour variants of the Ball Python have come on the market in the last few years. One of the most popular is without doubt the Jungle Ball Python, a variety in which yellow is intense. Albinos are also popular but there are even more rare varieties such as the caramel albino. The basic colour is nearly violet with yellow markings and black is absent. In contrast in melanistic animals black is dominant. Some melanistic Ball Pythons are virtually black. In so-called 'piebalds', part of the normal markings have been replaced by a snow-white blotch. This variant, which can also be found in the wild, has an asking price in the order of £ 6500 ($ 9500). *Python regius* is covered by the CITES Convention.

Python molurus bivittatus (Burmese Python)

A couple of sizes larger than the Ball Python is the Burmese Python. Only the sub species *Python molurus bivittatus* is kept in terrariums because *Python molurus molurus* is heavily protected.

Appearance

Whilst *Python molurus bivittatus* can reach lengths in excess of 234 in (6m) most individuals are less than 156 in (4m). They can rightly be classified as giant snakes with all the consequences for the size of the terrarium. The Burmese Python has a dark spear tip marking on its head that extends to the foremost part. Despite its size, the Python molurus bivittatus is known as being " friendly ". Be warned however, such large snakes can be dangerous.

The Burmese Python (*Python molurus bivittatus*) is a real giant amongst the giant snakes.]

Distribution

Python molurus bivittatus is found in Southeast Asia where it lives in wet areas. Its a good swimmer and often spends a considerable amount of time in water.

Housing

The terrarium needs to be large. Burmese Pythons can soak for days in water so the basin needs to be big enough and easy to clean. Although the animals don't

climb very much, any tree trunks provided need to be well anchored and capable of bearing the animals weight. During the day the temperature should be kept to between 80.5 and 89.5 degrees F (27 and 32 degrees C). Under the spot lamp the temperature can be allowed to rise to between 95 to 104 degrees F (35 and 40 degrees C). At night the temperature can be allowed to fall to about 71.5 degrees F (22 degrees C). Because this variety comes from wet areas its advisable to spray the terrarium regularly with tepid water.

Diet

Burmese Pythons are enthusiastic eaters and swallow rats and chickens alike. Rabbits are also on its menu. Prey is always strangled first.

Breeding

This variety is extremely easy to breed. From the beginning of December, gradually reduce the temperature to about 73.5 degrees F (23 degrees C) and reduce the relative air humidity to lower than normal. Simply reducing the amount of spraying can achieve this. Reduce the lighting time and feeding. It's preferable to separate the animals during this period.

Temperature and air humidity can be gradually increased from February. Feed the animals well before reuniting them. About a month after mating the female will stop eating. The eggs are laid approximately three months after mating. Make sure that a large tray lined with damp sphagnum moss or peat dust is placed in advance in the terrarium so that the female can lay her eggs. A clutch consists of between 13 and 35 eggs, but clutches of more than 100 eggs are not unknown.

A Burmese Python female incubates her young by coiling her tail loosely around the clutch. If the temperature in the clutch threatens to drop too much the animal will increase it slightly by muscular contractions. Incubation by the mother is generally less successful than by artificial means. Eggs that are artificially incubated at between 86 to 89.5 degrees F (30 to 32 degrees C) hatch after between 8 and 75 days. The majority of young are between 19.5 and 23.5 in (50 and 60 cm) long and weigh between 4.3 and 4.8 oz (120 and 135g).

Rearing

After the first moult, the young are already able to eat adult mice. They grow quickly reaching between 98.5 and 118 in (2.5 and 3 m) in length and about 44 lbs (20 kilos) in weight within 2 years.

Burmese Python albinos regularly become available for sale. Their care requirements are the same. *Python molurus bivittatus* also fall under the CITES law.

Various breeds of the Corn Snake can be bought. One of the best known is a variant that lacks black. The striped variety is also popular.

Elaphe guttata (Corn Snake)

The most widely kept snake is without doubt *Elaphe guttata*, the Corn Snake.

Appearance

Elaphe guttata is something of a canary amongst snakes. Red, orange, brown, black and sometime grey coloured snakes have been produced especially in the United States where the breeding of new colour varieties is very popular. Snake keepers in The Netherlands and Belgium have also become specialists in this branch of snake keeping. The belly is marked like a chessboard.

The record length of a corn snake is 72 in (1.82 m) but with an average length of between 31.5 and 47 in (80 and 120 cm) they are often considerably smaller.

Distribution

Elaphe guttata are found over large areas in the east and middle of the United States and in northeast Mexico. A few sub-species exist. In the wild they live both in damp and dry biotope.

Housing

This variety has no special requirements beyond one or two branches and a hide box (for example

a piece of tree bark, a tree stump or an upturned flowerpot). It's important to ensure that the terrarium is not damp otherwise the snake can develop pox. During the day the temperature should be maintained between 77 and 86 degrees F (25 and 30 degrees C). The heating can be switched off at night. Drinking water needs to be refreshed several times a day.

Diet

Elaphe guttata adapt to eating dead prey easily and are best fed on mice and young rats. Adult rats are too big. It's advisable though to separate animals when they are being fed to avoid the possibility of two snakes starting to eat the same prey. Without intervention there is a possibility that one snake will swallow the other together with the prey. Corn snakes strangle their prey before swallowing them. Some snakes will even strangle dead mice presented with tweezers just for good measure.

Sexing

It's not too difficult to determine sex as long as a number of animals of more or less the same size are available. Males have comparatively large tails that taper more gradually to the tip than in females. Young animals can be 'popped'. Probing, whereby a probe needle can be inserted further into the male than into the female, is also a possibility. (See chapter Breeding).

Breeding

Hibernation is advisable to stimulate animals to mate. But most Corn Snakes will reproduce without hibernation. Hibernation is actually beneficial to the health of the snake because it follows their natural living pattern in the wild. If the animals are woken early (for example in February) from hibernation, it's actually possible to obtain two clutches of eggs in one year although the second clutch is often smaller. On average, about eleven eggs are laid in the first clutch and about eight in the second, although clutches of 30 eggs have been known. With a temperature between 82.5 and 89.5 F (28 and 32 degrees C) the eggs hatch in 52 to 60 days. The eggs increase noticeably in weight and size during this period. Signs of the impending birth are visible when the eggs start to lose moisture and collapse. The young, usually between 8 and 13 in (20 and 33 cm) in length crawl out of their eggs a few days later.

Rearing

The young will eat baby mice after their first moulting. Unfortunately it often happens that the young don't start to eat independently. It sometimes helps to put a young snake and a baby mouse together in a box, for example a Tupperware box in which ventilation holes have been made. If this doesn't work then holding a baby mouse with a pair

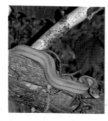

Elaphe taeniura friesei popularity winner amongst terrariums keepers

of tweezers and repeatedly tapping it against the snake's snout until it bites.

Young Elaphe guttata grow quickly. They can sometimes convert up to 40 percent of the weight of their prey to their own body weight. The majority of Corn Snakes are sexually mature at one and a half years old when they have reached a length of about 29.5 in (75 cm) and a weight close to 3.5 oz (100 g).

Availability

Elaphe guttata can be obtained in many varieties. Some are natural forms, such as the 'Okeetee'. These are animals with a lot of red pigmentation. The variety is named after a plantation in South Carolina where this red variety is common. Another natural variety is the Miami Face that has a typical red saddle marking on a grey background.

The striped Corn Snake is the

most popular of this breed, where the typical patch markings are replaced with lengthwise stripes. 'Blood red' defines a scarlet variant. Amelanistic Elaphe guttata are animals where the black lines are more or less missing. 'Frosted corns' look as though they are covered with a layer of frost. There are numerous other breeds including the albino. Even crosses with totally different varieties are obtainable. A cross between *Elaphe guttata* and *Lampropeltis getulus* is called 'Jungle Corn'

Family members
The subspecies Elaphe guttata emoryi occasionally come up for sale. This variety is more heavily built but shorter. The animals have the typical markings of the family but lack red and are brown/grey in colour.

In addition to *Elaphe guttata* there are numerous other *Elaphe* varieties that can be considered for a terrarium. Also originating from the south east of the United States is *Elaphe obsoleta*. This variety is more heavily built than *Elaphe guttata* but it's easier to care for. There are several sub-species, such as *E. obsoleta spiloides* (the Grey Rat Snake).

Elaphe bairdi comes from the dry areas in the south of Texas and northern Mexico. This variety used to be considered sub-specie of E. obsoleta, and it reaches a

length of between 39 and 55 in (100 and 140 cm) and must be kept in a dry terrarium.

The Elaphe family is also represented in Europe and Asia. The Amur Rat snake or Russian Rat snake *(Elaphe schrencki)* is one of the most well known Asiatic representatives. It can reach 59 inches (150 cm) in length and, just like the Corn Snake, is a very rewarding terrarium animal and needs the same care. Another Asian snake seen more and more frequently for sale is the *Elaphe taeniura*. This is without doubt a magnificent animal that can exceed 78 inches (2 m) in length.

The Amur Rat snake *(Elapse schrencki)* is a favourite with terrarium keepers.

Elaphe bairdi is a relatively infrequent terrarium inhabitant.

Heterodon nasicus
(Western Hognose)

Heterodon nasicus has a conspicuous appearance with its turned-up nose, which it thanks for its name.

Appearance
These are small animals, the majority of which grow no longer than 20 or 24 in (50 or 60 cm).

Distribution
They live in dry prairie areas in North America and mainly eat toads.

Diet
In captivity they usually eat mice without difficulty, although animals caught in the wild sometimes refuse this type of food (also see chapter Feeding). Their preference is for naked mice (pinkies).

Behaviour
Although they are not categorised as venomous snakes they are mildly poisonous but barely capable of injecting their venom with a bite. Nevertheless, care is advisable. Most people bitten by the Western Hognose didn't feel any symptoms even when the snake was intentionally allowed to chew on their hand. However, allergic reactions can produce sickness in those bitten.

In the wild at least the Western Hognose can be a comedian. When an enemy approaches and they feel threatened they will hiss loudly, flatten out their necks like a cobra and strike out as though attempting to bite. If the enemy has not taken to his heals after this display of force a completely different scenario unfolds. The Hognose turns on its back with its mouth open and tongue hanging out and plays dead. Should you pick up a supposedly "dead" Hognose it will simply hang limp. This behaviour is seldom if ever seen in the terrarium.

Housing
Due to its small size and inactive nature the Hognose only needs a small terrarium. They do however need to be able to hide, under a curved piece of bark for example. The animals like to dig so the substrata should be a few inches thick. I use a thick layer of woodchip.

During the day the temperature in the terrarium should be between 73.5 and 82.5 degrees F (23 and 28 degrees C). The heating can be turned off at night.

Breeding
Many Hognose refuse to eat from about autumn. This is an indication that they need to be allowed to hibernate which can be allowed to last for a few months without any concern. Once they have emerged from hibernation they are often greedy eaters. Mating takes place in the spring. Clutches of ten or so eggs are laid, which hatch after about 55 days.

The Western Hognose *(Heterodon nasicus)* remains small but is mildly poisonous

The African House Snake *(Lamprophis fuliginosus)* is mainly active at night

Rearing
The first moulting occurs unusually more or less immediately after the young hatch. Hognose snakes can then be fed with nestling mice (Pinky's). Some young eat these immediately. Their preference though is for dead prey. It can happen that having eaten straight away, young animals will stubbornly refuse all food. The trick of dipping a baby mouse in water that's held a frog generally works wonders.

Lamprophis fuliginosus (African House Snake)
Lamprophis fuliginosus also know as *Boaedon fuliginosus.*

Appearance
The brown *Lamprophis fuliginosus* grows to about 39 in (1m) in length.

Distribution
The house snake is a common, mainly nocturnal snake that's found over a large territory from East Africa to the Cape.

Housing
Snakes have few demands. A dry terrarium with a daytime temperature of between 82.5 and 86 degrees F (28 and 30 degrees C), a little cooler at night is sufficient. Provide a hide, for example an upturned flowerpot with a hole in it or a piece of bark that they can crawl under. The animals prefer to be out of sight during the daytime. A small drinking dish completes the furnishing.

Diet
House snakes are voracious eaters. It's a good idea to feed the

Lampropeltis
mexicana s less
extravagantly colou-
red than most other
Lampropeltis varie-
ties

animals separately because jealou-
sy during feeding is not uncom-
mon. Their menu consists mainly
of mice even though in the wild
they will also try reptiles, birds
and bird eggs.

Breeding
Lamprophis fuliginosus is possibly
the easiest snake to breed. 'Just
like chickens', a breeder once
said. Somebody who was buying
a couple of house snakes in a pet
shop asked what he had to do to
breed them: 'Nothing' was the
answer. 'They've probably already
mated in the bag between Africa
and here.'

Anybody who is serious about
breeding would do well to make a
permanent laying box available
for the eggs. This can best be a
tray lined with damp peat dust or
sphagnum moss. At a temperature
of between 73.5 and 86 degrees F
(23 and 30 degrees C) eggs will
hatch between 77 and 87 days.
The young measure 7 to 10 in (18
to 25 cm) and eat nestling mice
mostly without any problem at all.

Lampropeltis getulus (King Snake)

King Snakes are sturdy animals
that are very much at home in a
terrarium.

Appearance
Some sub species of *Lampropeltis
getulus* are sometimes difficult to
tell apart. The majority are black

or brown and have white or yellow stripes. The sub-species
Lampropeltis getulus holbrooki
has spots over its entire body
but the most colourful is
Lampropeltis getulus californiae.
Young from the same nest can
have completely different colouring from each other. One may
have a white stripe lengthways
over its back for example while
another has a diagonal stripe.
Lampropeltis getulus can grow to
an average of 59 in (150 cm) in
length with, exceptions of up to
70 in (180 cm).

Distribution
King Snakes live in various bio-
topes in the south of the United
States – from desert areas to coni-
fer forests – where they hunt small
rodents, birds, lizards and snakes.

Housing
Lampropeltis getulus has no special
requirements. A hide made of branches and a couple of large pieces of
well-anchored stone is sufficient.
The daytime temperature may vary
between 75.5 and 86 degrees F (24
and 30 degrees C). At night the
temperature may be allowed to
drop to between 64.5 and 68
degrees F (18 and 20 degrees C).

Diet
Lampropeltis getulus eats snakes
as part its own diet so it's a good
idea to keep them on their own in
a terrarium. If you want to keep
several together they should be of

Lampropeltis triangu-
lum annulata much
sought after because
of its clear colouring

approximately the same size. Separate them during feeding to avoid any risks.

Breeding

Breeding *Lampropeltis getulus* is relatively easy. Let the animals hibernate for about two to three months, after which mating takes place. During mating, the male often attaches himself to the female by biting into her neck without this leading to injury.

Research with 25 *Lampropeltis getulus* pairs revealed that mating lasts an average of 4.3 hours. The longest recorded mating lasted 6.5 hours. Eggs hatch at the earliest 37 days and at the latest 58 days following fertilisation. The incubation temperature must be between 71.5 and 86 degrees F (22 and 30 degrees C). The young are between 10 and 11.5 inches (25 and 29 cm) in length when they emerge from the egg.

Lampropeltis getulus californiae is the albino variety and very popular

Thamnophis sirtalis parietalis

Thamnophis sirtalis tetrataenia

Rearing

Rearing the young produces few problems. After the first moulting, they eat baby mice. In the first year of life, they moult about ten times, after which the largest may have reached a length of 27.5 in (70 cm). By that time they will have easily consumed seventy young mice.

Relatives

The *Lampropeltis* family consists of more varieties that are kept in terrariums. The Milk snakes *(Lampropeltis triangulum)* are especially popular. The diverse subspecies are beautifully coloured. They have brilliant red, black and yellow bands running over their bodies. The care required does not differ to that of *Lampropeltis getulus*. This applies also to other King Snake varieties such as *Lampropeltis pyromelana*, L. zonata en L. mexicana, which are all attractively coloured snakes.

Thamnophis sirtalis (Common Garter Snake)

Garter snakes have been one of the most widely kept varieties for some years. Unfortunately the popularity of these snakes has reduced considerably in the last few years, but this is completely unjustified because the majority of the species and sub-species are beautiful to look at and very lively. Being stamped a 'beginners snake' has possibly had an effect since most enthusiasts choose snakes with more allure. Of the Garter Snakes available for sale *Thamnophis sirtalis* is the most common. The sub-species *Thamnophis sirtalis parietalis* is also often to be obtained.

Appearance

These black or green snakes mostly have 3 light lengthwise stripes (the garters). A number of varieties also display patch patterns. *Thamnophis sirtalis* grows to a maximum of 51 in (130 cm) in length and often has red spots or black patches between the stripes.

Distribution

Garter snakes are a successful animal group. In North America they cover an enormous area living by lakes, streams, in grasslands and forests. Some varieties are real followers of culture and even live in city parks and gardens.

Housing

The terrarium for a Garter Snake does not need to be too big because most varieties don't grow larger than 39 in (1m). A terrarium of about 31.5 in long by 16 in (80 cm by 40 cm) high and wide is large enough for a single adult animal. During the day the temperature should remain between 71.5 and 82.5 degrees F (22 and 28 degrees C). At night the temperature may be allowed to drop by 41 to 50 degrees F (five to ten degrees C).

Although Garter Snakes are often to be found in and near water, the terrarium may not be damp. Garter snakes do best in a dry terrarium in which a water dish is placed, in which they can soak. A water dish with between 1.5 to 2.5 pints (approximately 1 to 1.5 litres) of water is sufficient. Don't fill the dish up to the edge or it will overflow when the snake gets in.

The substrate can consist of rough woodchips. Add a hide in the form of a curved piece of bark or a tree stump and the furnishing is complete. To make the whole effect generally more attractive, one or two artificial plants can be added. Real plants can not be considered because they will be easily damaged under the snake's weight. There is also a danger that they could produce too high an air humidity. Thamnophis are very sensitive to excessive moisture and could be frequently troubled by blisters (Pox), especially if a floor is damp.

Diet

Feeding Garter Snakes presents no problems. Live and dead fish can be given. Goldfish and guppies are suitable amongst others. Frozen smelt is available at pet shops. Once thawed out in warm water this fish variety is a delicacy for the Garter Snake. Some varieties of fish contain a large amount of thiamin, an enzyme that destroys Vitamin B1. Garter snakes are especially susceptible to this so it's advisable to add a

vitamin supplement to the fish. If this is forgotten, the snake may eventually suffer from a vitamin B1 deficiency. The initial symptoms manifest themselves with the snake making uncontrollable rearward jerking movements with its head. In a later stage the snake rapidly turns its body like a corkscrew. It's important to give vitamin B1 the moment the symptoms first appear. Experience showed that dissolving vitamin B1 tablets in water and giving the solution to the snake with a pipette proved to be the best method. The animal involved received a few drops three to four days in a row and recovered completely.

Thamnophis sirtalis parietalis

Thamnophis sirtalis sirtalis is possibly the most frequently kept Garter Snake

Nerodia fasciata

Breeding
In general, these animals breed readily in a terrarium. Hibernatio stimulates them to mate. Mating mostly occurs immediately after leaving the hibernation place in March or April but an increase in the terrarium temperature and in the lighting time can achieve the same result.

The sperm have a remarkably lon life. It often happens that after mating the female will store the sperm only to fertilise the eggs the following spring. Scientific research has shown that the sperm can remain fertile for up to 58 months.

The gestation period of the Garte snake is to a large extent dependent upon external circumstances the most important of which is temperature. As a guideline for animals kept in a terrarium, the gestation period is two and a half to three months. The birth announces itself as the female gets noticeably fatter and starts to look for warm spots. Just before the birth she also become restless Garter snakes give birth to live young mostly in the summer or a the beginning of the autumn. The number of young varies enormously but it can be up to eighty. Unfortunately, relatively few of the litter survive.

A valuable supplement to the Garter snake's menu is earthworms. Although they don't eat just any variety, the *Thamnophis sirtalis* loves them. Earthworms can be bought at a pet shop but if you have a garden you can easily catch them yourself. Make sure though that the worms don't come from an area contaminated by insecticides.

Many Garter snakes eat small mice. Because the faeces produced by mice smell less strongly than those produced from eating fish many enthusiasts feed their animals mice which are actually more nourishing. To get the snakes used to mice, smear them with fish. Mice can also be given in a dish mixed for example with a little thawed smelt.

Sexing
It's not normally difficult to sex Garter snakes. Females are visibly sturdier and their tails narrow earlier.

Rearing
The young eat the same food as